My Pets

My Goldfish

By Pamela Walker

Children's Press®
A Division of Scholastic Inc.
New York / Toronto / London / Auckland / Sydney
Mexico City / New Delhi / Hong Kong
Danbury, Connecticut

Photo Credits: Cover, pp. 5, 7, 9, 11, 13, 15, 17, 19, 21 by Maura Boruchow
Contributing Editor: Jeri Cipriano
Book Design: Nelson Sa

Library of Congress Cataloging-in-Publication Data

Walker, Pamela, 1958-
  My Goldfish / by Pamela Walker.
    p. cm.—(My pets)
  Includes bibliographical references and index.
  ISBN 0-516-23185-5 (lib. bdg.)—ISBN 0-516-23288-6 (pbk.)
  1. Goldfish—Juvenile literature. [1. Goldfish. 2. Pets.] I. Title. II. My pet (Children's Press)

  SF458.G6 W32 2000
  639.3'7484—dc21   00-031632

Contents

See my new pet?

This is my **goldfish**.

I will name my
goldfish Goldie.

My goldfish has **gills.**

Gills help fish breathe in water.

My goldfish has **fins.**

Fins help fish swim.

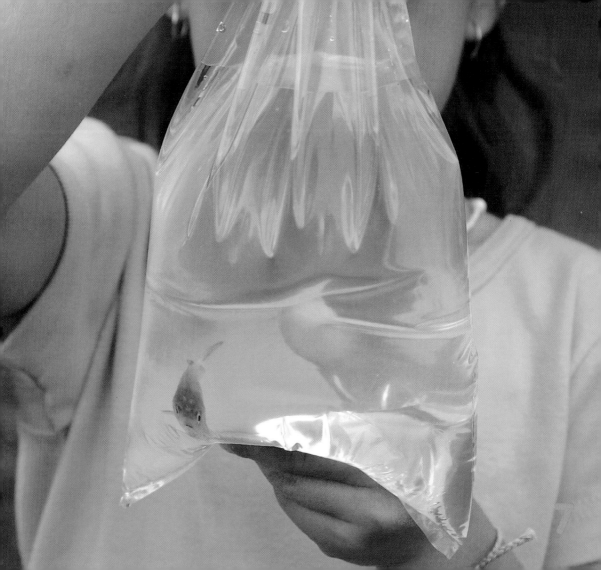

I have a tank for Goldie.

The tank is her home.

9

I put rocks at the bottom of the tank.

I put a plant in the tank, too.

Goldie swims in her new home.

Sometimes Goldie hides behind the plant.

13

I feed Goldie goldfish food.

Goldie swims up to eat
the food.

Sometimes I have to put clean water in the tank.

I use a **net** to take Goldie out of the tank.

I try not to scare Goldie.

I put Goldie in a bowl.

I take some dirty water out of the tank.

Then I add clean water.

Today I got a new goldfish.

Now Goldie has a friend.

What name should I give my new goldfish?

21

New Words

fins (**finz**) parts of a fish
that help it to swim

gills (**gihlz**) parts of a fish
that help it to breathe
in water

goldfish (**gold**-fish) a small
orange or gold fish

net (**net**) something used

to catch a fish

To Find Out More

Books

Goldfish Hide-and-Seek
by Satoshi Kitamura
Farrar, Straus & Giroux

Me and My Pet Fish
by Christine Morley and Carole Orbell
World Book

Your First Goldfish
by Mariana Gilbert
TFH Publications

Web Site

The Goldfish Sanctuary
http://www.petlibrary.com/goldfish/fishcare.htm
On this site, you can find out what you need
to know about caring for goldfish.

Index

About the Author
Pamela Walker lives in Brooklyn, New York.

Reading Consultants
Kris Flynn, Coordinator, Small School District Literacy,
The San Diego County Office of Education

Shelly Forys, Certified Reading Recovery Specialist,
W.J. Zahnow Elementary School, Waterloo, IL

Peggy McNamara, Professor, Bank Street College of
Education, Reading and Literacy Program